I0483567

Top Business Skills You Need To Master

What Your Business Skills Say About You and How to Small Talk into Persuasion

By

Thomas Eriksson

eCare Publishing *Copyright* © 2015

Table of Contents

Check Out Our Other Books @ ecarepublishing.com

Introduction

Learn which skills are effective to running a persuasive meeting and create alliances, increase sales, delegate responsibility and list the goals you want to achieve. Business demands certain skills and the understanding of how to accomplish what matters. Easily discover the tools successful business people use to come out on top!

What do you think your business skills say about you in this moment? Do you feel confident in your business skills? Have you already determined areas you could improve? Your business skills are imperative to your success. Any successful business person such as Warren Buffet, Donald Trump, Oprah Winfrey, and Bill Gates reached their goals and became experts because of their abilities in business and in persuasive small talk.

Discover ways for you to reach the goals you have set forth by assessing your skills, gaining new skills, and finding out what other successful individuals have done.

The main principles of business apply to any industry, from how to create alliances to delegating responsibilities. Once you have the basic skills, you will be able to apply them to the industry you are going to work in.

You can use this book to gain the skills you do not have and help your current idea come to fruition. Many people have amazing business ideas, many of which you may never hear about because they lack the ability to make a business successful.

Donald Trump has filed for bankruptcy at least twice, if not more over his long career as a successful businessman. His most recent issue rests in Atlantic City with a casino. At the beginning, Atlantic City was going strong for casinos and casino owners and investors, but economic troubles closed in, turning a successful business into a bankrupt casino, which was then sold to another investor.

It can happen to anyone; however, the key to success is not to give up on all of your ideas. Where one idea might not lead to success, another can. You not only have to have the determination to succeed, but the skills to make it happen. If you lack the necessary business skills to get noticed, gain investors, or bring together a solid team—then failure is the result. As you read along, you will gain the insights to developing winning business skills.

« Chapter 1 »

Evaluate Your Skills

Being in business as a CEO, manager, owner, CFO or in any other leadership position within a company requires you have certain skills, the ability to keep up with the changing times, legal aspects, and that you have confidence in yourself. Before you can begin to gain the skills you need in business, you must first assess your strengths and weaknesses. What is your current management ability? If you have accepted a new position or are starting a new company, what skills do you need to develop for this career?

To evaluate your skills you need to honestly assess your own performance and examine ways you can improve on the skills you require for your career. You should look at the needs of the business you are in, the management activity, and education required. When you were hired for the position or as you seek a position, there is always a job description you can read that outlines the skills, knowledge, and education needed to obtain the position. Start with the information in the job description as a way to evaluate what you have, what you may lack, and your strengths/weaknesses in those areas.

What you should do in any job

Any position you have ever had is going to evaluate your knowledge, skills, strengths, and weaknesses. You can monitor your performance through these evaluations, as well as assess your own thoughts on your performance.

Think of a time you dealt with a difficult client or customer. Were you able to persuade that person, or diffuse their anger (depending on the situation you think of)? During this exchange, what could you have said or done that would have been more effective? Was there a weakness in your communication, listening, or evaluation of the situation?

Besides feedback from your management and bosses, you need to obtain regular feedback on your performances from others. Feedback can come from clients, customers and other employees at the same level as you, friends, family, and acquaintances.

Once you assess examples, obtain feedback and look at your performance in an objective, third party assessment, describe (in writing) and analyze improvements that need to be made.

The key to being effective in any business, whether you are just starting out as an employee or reaching a CEO position is to maintain and grow your knowledge and understanding of the industry. To be effective in your role, sharpening your skills and knowledge is a non-stop process.

Remain flexible in your position. If changes are required by the home office, be flexible enough to try these new approaches and recommendations. The new requirements may not work, but until you have tried them and proven that the older method was more effective, you truly cannot say there is an issue with the new concepts.

Set personal goals in your career. A personal development plan, with frequent updates for new achievements will keep you motivated at work and help you improve your performance.

Gathering the skills you require

No one is perfect. Even successful business moguls like Warren Buffet, Donald Trump, Bill Gates, Larry Page, Mark Zuckerberg, Liliane Bettencourt and Richard Branson had their struggles. They worked up from the bottom and became savvy business people by knowing their strengths, weaknesses, and creating a team that would complement their skills.

You do need to keep up with changes of time by reading the Wall Street Journal, Business Weekly, and similar media. You need to know what micro and macro economics are, and how to assess them. It will take time to keep up with the changes, but with training and practice you can remain on top of the knowledge in order to assess the skills you need to improve on, or the people you need to gather to maintain the company.

Hiring people that complement your strengths and weaknesses ensures you have a complete management team that can handle the various business situations you may find yourself in. With a an effective management team structure, you will have someone who is persuasive for meetings, a person strong in sales, and a company filled with employees who can help you reach your business goals.

Working on skills you do not have

Education should never stop. It is impossible to know everything because improvements, new concepts, ideas, and innovations are made every day. If you are just starting out as a regular low level employee, you will need to prepare your education. Determine what courses you need for your personal goals, as well as the skills you require to become a top level employee. Get involved in extracurricular activities and organizations where you can volunteer.

For business, whether you are just starting out in a new position, or starting your own company, showing that you are a part of your community through volunteering and extracurricular activities will set you apart.

Even if you have already graduated with a degree, been working in a company for 10 years, and recently moved into management or started your own company, you can always better prepare yourself with further education. Online courses; taking a night course at your local university, and reading will help you develop the skills you need, but do not have.

Communication skills are imperative in any business and career. During your time in school you can sharpen your skills for communication by taking public speaking courses. It is also best to take a Dale Carnegie style course in communication. Dale Carnegie courses are available online and in many states. There are courses and seminars for communication, as well as leadership training, corporate solutions, and additional training options.

The place you obtain additional training is as important as the university you have chosen for your beginning education. Clients, competition, and your peers will recognize your skills when the skills come from a well-known training facility.

If you want to come out on top, with recognition for your business acumen, then it is imperative that you evaluate your skills honestly, complement your skills with a team who helps shore up your strengths and weakness, and have the training necessary.

« Chapter 2 »

Communication Skills

In business, communication skills are going to stand between you and your ultimate success. Every person, from employees to potential clients you deal with, will require a certain set of communication skills. Some employees and clients will need more persuasion than others. There are five skills that are beneficial in business:

- Listening to others perspectives

- Letting the person know you are listening

- Persuading individuals based on the person and situation

- Written communication

- Customer service

Listening to employees, clients, and management teams will help you see their perspective. You have your own opinions, but listening from the "shoes" of another can help you understand their perspective.

Anyone who has worked as a cashier in a retail store, even for a short period of time, will understand the importance of listening from others' perspectives. A cashier position in the Dollar Store, Wal-mart, Kmart, or a mall in the store gives you a unique perspective for any business. It also helps you develop a thick skin for customer service and how to handle various employee situations as you work your way up the ladder.

Cold calling for surveys or being on a customer service telephone line as a company representative are two other ways to obtain a unique perspective on how to be a better communicator.

Individuals in these positions deal with irate customers. Phone customer service representatives often have at least one customer who swears at them, hangs up angrily, yells, or is derogatory throughout the entire call. The justification is not there to take it out on the one who received the call; however, it happens. In this position, a skilled listener is able to see the person's perspective, take the anger in stride, and learn more about the caller than if they tried to interrupt the tirade.

Successful business people know that you can learn more by listening than by talking. By listening, you hear the emotions, the words, and by observing the client or employee in person you are able to read body language cues. You are going to work with all types of people, which is why you need to be able to listen, observe, and then communicate in an effective manner.

From a management to employee perspective

Working with employees, means you will work with a variety of people, who need to be motivated to work in different ways. Some of your employees may need more coaching to continue working effectively, while others may need less interference to work successfully. Again, listening and observing helps you determine how to approach your employees to ensure everyone is working to the best of their abilities. Your employees are there to help with the advancement of your business and they have skills that will help with this. Without employees you will have to do all the work yourself.

Offering clients what they need

Communication with clients, competition, or acquaintances that can help your business succeed will require the same listening skills used in a slightly different way. The goal is different when you speak with clients, the competition, and acquaintances—it is for the advancement of your business because that person has something you need. It may be funding, sales, or media portals that the person has access to. You need clients, you need to assess your competition, and you need to make sure people recognize your business.

Written communication

Sales and marketing go hand in hand, and it is a topic for later discussion. However, one marketing point is to have effective written communication skills to get your sales pitch across. The wrong usage of words, miss-spellings, and errors in written communication can affect your reputation with both clients and employees.

Being Persuasive in your Communications

Whether you are hosting a meeting, creating marketing copy, or trying to create alliances, you need to have some persuasive techniques in your arsenal.

A local businessman from Grand Rapids stated, "the best way to be persuasive is to understand the subject completely, have no if's or perhaps' in your conversation, and understand who you are being persuasive with."

It does not matter if you are speaking with employees, or potential clients for whom you are trying to create an alliance with, or holding a meeting. You need to understand the subject inside and out to avoid any issues. As you study a subject in order to talk about it, you also need to consider the questions that may be asked.

An exercise:

To understand the subject you will be speaking about, consider viewing the subject from your client, employee, or another person's perspective. Analyze the information as if it was the first time you were hearing it and seeing it. What if you were talking with someone who had no idea what your business is about? How would you explain the information and what would you like to know?

One of the vaults in communication and being persuasive in any setting is for the person to view their subject from only their perspective. Someone else may be just as intelligent on the subject, but until you look at it from a novice standpoint, you may not be able to understand and be ready to field any of the questions you may be asked.

Looking at the subject from several perspectives ensures you have no "if's" and "perhaps'" statements in your phrases. You will eliminate the need for fillers such as "um." The more fluent you are in your speech, the more someone will feel you know the subject.

You also have to understand why. Why is someone going to be interested in what you are persuading them into? What benefit does it give the listener in the meeting, or any conversation you engage in, to be persuaded, one way or another by what you have to say? Makes sure you understand the "why" before you try to make someone else listen and accept what you are saying.

Last thoughts on persuasion

A good persuader is someone who does not give an order, but persuades a person without the person realizing they are being led into the decision the persuader wants.

You might want to read articles on psychopaths, from a psychopath's perspective. This is suggested not for the criminal aspect, but on the persuasion techniques used by these individuals. Many psychopaths are able to persuade a person without their conscious knowledge because there are no orders and the "sales" techniques are so charismatic that it happens with little effort.

To become a better persuader you can also take courses that help you learn persuasive techniques, examine different management styles that allow for a more persuasive manner, and keep reading to find new techniques.

For your business and client meetings, it is important to know what the client needs, respect your client, and develop your persuasive techniques. If you need to you can hire someone who has the natural charisma and persuasive skills required.

Remember these points:

- Always listen to your client, employee, or the person you are trying to persuade

- Understand the person's needs

- Hold frequent meetings or surveys to evaluate how you are doing with meeting client needs and see where you can become more persuasive

It takes time to learn persuasion skills, if they do not come natural. It also takes training and practice. Whenever you have conversations with anyone – from a friend to a client, practice your persuasive training and skills.

« Chapter 3 »

Create Alliances

You know you need to evaluate yourself, gain skills to be an effective business leader, and persuade those around you through communication, as well as have superior communication skills for all aspects of your life. Now you need to take the skills you have developed or are developing in order to create alliances.

Who do you need to create alliances with?

- Professional organizations

- Attorneys

- Accountants

- Media

- Clients

- Competition

- Employees

- Decision Makers

- Gatekeepers

Professional Organizations

Professional organizations such as the Better Business Bureau, Chamber of Commerce, and the Small Business Association, are necessary alliances. Even if you work for a large brand name company as a manager, CEO, or other executive you still need to be recognized by these professional organizations. These organizations help locals find what they require from a business or business person. The name of the game is to get your brand recognized and be considered the go-to company of your local area, and possibly on a national basis. For local alliances, the organizations listed will go to the person that immediately comes to mind for what a client or visitor requires. You want to be the person they go to when it applies to the business you are in.

Attorneys and Accountants

Attorneys and accountants are two trusted individuals. Someone who is going to handle legal matters or money for another has to be trustworthy. Instead of turning to a neighbor for a suggestion, it is more often than not the accountant or attorney that is asked "do you know a person who works in such and such industry?" Since attorneys and accountants know they are going to be asked these questions, they often have people they recommend. Additionally, it can be a person they work for as an accountant or as an attorney. You want to know as many people in this industry as you can, but they also need to be someone you trust to give you a recommendation. Your reputation depends on the people you know, thus the person giving you a recommendation has to be worthy of offering it.

Media

Media alliances are imperative on a local and national level. Who does someone turn to when the country's economics are suffering, particularly in the transportation industry? Warren Buffet is one person usually being interviewed with regards to the economy, transportation, and certain stock movements. He is considered a leading expert in business. In your local area, you want to be that person. You want a media representative to come to you when they need statistics or information regarding your industry. If they can turn to you, then you are getting free advertising. A guest appearance on a TV show, radio show, in magazines or newspapers, means someone is hearing or reading about you.

Clients

Current and former clients are also people to create alliances with. Depending on your type of business you may satisfy a client's need and they may not need your services again. Highly unlikely, but your business is like this, you can still keep client details as a way to use them for alliances. Clients are people in business too, whether they own a company or are a gatekeeper to a decision maker you need to reach. Not every client will be useful, but it is always a good idea to keep them in the back of your mind should you come upon a situation where you may need them.

Gatekeepers and Decision Makers

Gatekeepers are executive assistances, secretaries, plant foremen's, and others who stand in front of the decision makers. They are the people that will let you see the person you truly need to speak to. If you cannot get past the gatekeeper to make an appointment, then you won't get what you need. Gatekeepers can also be under-appreciated, or feel that they are, so making sure you take a few moments to learn about them by speaking with them, and even sending them a holiday card can help you later on when you need the decision maker. In some instances, the gatekeeper is the right hand person to the decision maker. This person's opinion could be just as valuable to the decision maker as their own, which would determine if your needs are going to be met.

Decision makers typically work at businesses you need to secure as helpers to your industry. It may be a client you are trying to gain for your company. There is also another type of decision maker that you may need to be a part of your business—the competition.

Competition

Sometimes the people you are in competition with can be the best alliances you have. Every business has a time when they need competition, whether it is to gain insight into the business models, to be acquaintances for the express purpose of meeting the people you need to know, or to share clients. What would happen if you need to serve a new client, but you cannot take on anyone else? Perhaps you own a construction company and have five houses to build, but a new client wants you to start on their home now? If you know the competition, you can recommend the client go to this other person for their needs. The client will remember this and should they need your services again, they may try to come back. The one thing you gain—is the client you had to turn away will remember you still helped them in some capacity. The person will talk to others about how professional and helpful you were, even though you could not take them on as a client. But, you first have to have a competitor you are willing to have a relationship with.

Employees

Employees are also people you need to have alliances with. It is more than a matter of ensuring they work well for you. Your employee could be married to someone you need to establish an alliance with. For example, you might own a business office that needs repairs and an employee is married to a general contractor you want to use. It might be the employee is family to a competitor, media agency, or professional organization. You never want to discount employees and the alliances you can create with them and through them for the betterment of your business.

Business Surveys

Many larger corporations conduct surveys. While it might seem that a survey would be obsolete in this day and age with social media, surveys actually hold a lot of power when it comes to alliances that will help you increase sales. Surveys conducted every quarter or annually can be used by media as a way of promoting your business. More importantly, for this chapter, business surveys help you create those alliances. Someone can look at your survey, media post, and information and then decide to use your company versus another, ensuring you secure the alliance you are trying to create.

« Chapter 4 »

Increase Sales

Sales and marketing are a symbiotic pairing in the business world. For you to increase sales, you must first create alliances and now you know who to target for those relationships. The ways to create sales have not changed in terms of older methods, but there are new methods to add to your sales techniques.

- Word of Mouth

- Media

- Professional Organizations

- Your Reputation

- The Business' Reputation

- Social Media

- Websites

- Exceeding Client Expectations

- Company Goals

- Competition and Pricing

- Gatekeepers

Word of Mouth

Word of mouth is the most important sales technique any company has ever had or will have. There are different methods within the concept of word of mouth, discussed in a bit; however, as a generalized topic—word of mouth through communication is essential. Remember those persuasive communication skills you learned? They are going to come in handy for your sales. The more subtly persuasive you are the more sales you can make. This is also again where teams of employees are very helpful. You have employees who are on the front lines making the business more and more sales, and you have managers overseeing them, and you as well as each of these important people have to do their part to further drive sales and create a continuum of success. Happy employees are going to talk about where they work. Those who love their jobs are going to help you advertise your business.

Media

Radio and other media can be a way to freely advertise if you do it correctly. This goes back to creating the proper alliances and surveys. When the media receives the survey your company conducts each quarter, half a year, or annually, it will get filed. If you have created proper alliances, then your media alliance will look at your information, call you when they have a topic you can be an expert on, and you get to advertise you and your company. It all boils down to having the reputation and your personal name that is worth your alliances remembering. Anytime you get to advertise, you have just increased your potential for more sales.

Professional Organizations

These alliances are also your way to more sales. The attorneys, accountants, Chamber of Commerce, Better Business Bureau, and Small Business Administration are all going to help spread your company name around—due to your alliance. It goes back to having the reputation where the person at one of these professional organizations will mention you above your competition. Other professional organizations can be found through volunteer work and extracurricular activities. Your hobbies can lead you to more people and professional organizations that are willing to talk about your company and you, which lead to sales.

Your Reputation

Throughout this chapter, your reputation has been mentioned. You, personally, need to maintain a reputation in your business circle that others view as professional and worth doing business with. Your personal reputation as a professional in your industry can be a path to generating more sales. Every time you meet someone new you can pass out your business card, explain what you do, and ensure the person sees you as an expert in your field. Media can also help establish you, personally, as an expert in addition to any company you work for.

The Business' Reputation

Every employee has a responsibility for maintaining their company's reputation. The business' reputation is also built on knowing the competition, knowing the market inside and out, and looking for ways you can increase your market share. It may mean hiring good sales people, a sales and marketing team, and knocking on doors. Knocking on doors may seem an antiquated method, considering the internet options we have today, however, it still works. It's the reason many companies send flyers around to apartment complexes and homes. Nothing is going to replace relationships when it comes to establishing a business reputation that you can make sales on.

Social Media

Social media works for a select few. There are hundreds of thousands of websites online today and they are all vying for a spot on social media. Recent studies suggest that less than half a business' sales come from social media, unless it is a brand name that is already recognized. You do want to use social media, including Facebook, Twitter, Wordpress, RSS feeds, and other outlets, but you cannot depend on it completely for your sales.

iMedia Connection is just one of many companies that surveyed social media and sales. The result shows for new companies, social media is less effective in obtaining sales. Furthermore, unless a company is well branded, social media gets lost in the sea of numerous competitors.

The trouble with social media is many social media users are in passive mode. They are on to check updates of people they know, with only some time concentrated on looking at businesses and making purchases. Those who are in task oriented mode are going to be your main sales through social media.

A person who is online to shop may conduct an internet search using keywords and happen upon your social media site before your website due to updated, fresh content. It ensures a sale occurs; however, the person can be just as likely to avoid the social media page for your competitor's website.

Websites

A website for your business is essential for increasing sales. It must be user-friendly, offer transparency in what you do and offer, and explain things in detail. You never want the who, what, why, how, when, and where left unanswered. Your website will generate sales as long as people know how to find it and it is easy to use.

This is an area where you may need to hire an expert team. While the internet professes to have an easy method to launch a website; it is actually much harder than you think. It takes listing your site in a search directory, gaining momentum to make sales, and keeping up with new content. Running a land based business plus an online site, is time consuming. Your time may be better spent delegating this project to an outside company—there again it is about the right alliances, whether you use an internal employee or separate company.

Exceeding Client Expectations

Clients have expectations; however, if you want to increase sales you need to exceed any expectation they will have. When you go above and beyond what the client expects, they talk with their friends, family, and anyone else who will listen. Being an authority in your business is the first step to exceeding client expectations. Remember how you need to communicate about your company in order to persuade clients to join you in the first place? Here is where you put all of that knowledge into practice. You utilize your knowledge to not only explain your company, but to exceed your client's expectations on what you truly know.

For instance, you might sell construction tools. You may have only one brand, although there are several out there. A client may walk in expecting you to know everything about your brand. You can exceed their expectations by knowing about others and how they compare. You may discuss your tool then follow it up with a different brand stating your drill provides more uses because you can exchange the heads from a drill to a saw and again to a light. Another brand may require the client to purchase three tools instead of a 3-in-1 tool.

Knowing about your product is expected. Knowing about other products, components, or accessories may not be expected. This is just one method that you can use to exceed a client's perception of you and your business.

Another good example is a retail company. You sell hundreds of different products. More than a year ago, a client bought a product and it has broken. The warranty has expired and there is no replacement part for the broken section of the product. Instead, of saying sorry there is nothing I can do, you have the ability to give them the amount they paid you for the product. They can then use this money in your store or elsewhere. Maybe today you did not make a new sale with the money you returned to the client; however, you know you have just earned their loyalty.

Company Goals

Employees need sales goals. Your company structure needs to allow for sales goals by providing enough information for your employees to make a sale. It is often helpful to ask your employees, managers, and further up the ladder what sales goals are achievable in their eyes. There should be short and long term goals established. Once the goals have been established, they need to be shared with all levels, throughout the company so that every staff member has a purpose above and beyond sales. Weekly up to yearly goals should be set, with rewards as a motivator. Cash rewards are the best motivator to increase sales; however, you also need to remain within your yearly budget. Other options include pizza parties, bringing lunch to your employees, summer and winter parties, and an end of year bonus. You and your employees need to have personal and business' goals that incentivize everyone on the entire team to achieve these goals.

Competition and Pricing

Business is dependent on the competition, as well as the price you have on your goods or services. You do need to know what your competitors offer and at what price. It used to be you could have a guarantee on your goods and services, where you would return the clients funds— no questions asked. A lot of companies have started doing this again. You may need to find other methods to set yourself apart from the competition besides pricing. It might be a special 2 for 1 sale in the middle of summer, where you know all your competition only offers sales during the holiday season.

Undercutting your sales prices to make it against the competition is not always the correct move to increase sales. You might sell more at 50% off, but in the end you make the same amount in sales. The type of business you are a part of will determine the competition and pricing scenarios you need to draft.

Gatekeepers

Creating alliances with gatekeepers is just the beginning. Those who hold the keys to people you need to speak with also stand in the way of making new sales. Perhaps it is the executive assistant to the media liaison or client you hope to bring over from the competition. Until you can get past this person to the one you need, you cannot make the sale you are hoping for. It is after all, the reason you created an alliance with them in the first place.

Above all, the only way to increase sales is to ensure you have something clients want. As long as you have a supply that is in demand, you have the potential to increase sales.

« Chapter 5 »

Delegate Responsibilities

Delegation is one of the hardest things to do in a business. Many managers do not reach lofty heights because they are afraid to work. However, there comes a time when you no longer have the time to take on all of the projects that need to get done. Consider the construction example again.

A general contractor cannot sustain a comfortable life building one home at a time. The general contractor needs to have multiple projects they oversee. It requires construction crews, with a leading person at each site, and laborers to do the grunt work. Delegating the responsibilities is necessary. This frees up the owner or overall manager to check each site, contact clients, and find more projects or ways to make more sales.

If you are not a person comfortable with delegating, then you will need to learn. Yes, you are going to have the overall responsibility, but if you structure your department, company, or team with members you trust, it makes it much easier to delegate.

You definitely need to have employees with the skills to take on the tasks you delegate. Once you have the team, your work in delegating is not done; you still need to do the following:

- Delegate the work appropriately

- Trust the person to get the task completed

- Coach employees based on how they work

- Monitor the person at each stage

Delegate work appropriately

Every company has a sensitive information security structure, with regards to what information can and cannot be shared and with whom. A back office cashier is not someone who has the security from home office to work on budget reports, so delegating to a person in a correct position for that work is imperative.

The person may be able to handle the work without question and you may wish to delegate the work because you trust them; however, you also have to maintain the company rules in sharing information.

There is a delicate balance in delegating correctly. You have to follow the proper chain of command, and be careful not to tread on others. There is a respect to the company hierarchy. A low level manager may have the ability to do a project, but the person directly under you may be the person that should be assigned that work.

When you delegate the responsibility, make certain the employee has an understanding as to why you needed to delegate the task. Yes to a degree it is their job to take on any task you assign; however, there can also be trust issues from your employees.

Trust the person to get the task completed

Besides trusting the person to handle the task you delegate, there is a certain amount of trust you need to place in that person to get the task completed on time. Some employees need more overseeing than others. If you need to incentivize one employee more than another with words, then do so; using the right words will work. Taking the time to compliment an employee on their work and letting them know you trust them to complete the task will help ensure the task gets done on time.

As you have to trust your employee, your employee also has to trust you. An employee that sees you delegate a task, and then go over to another employee of an equal level, and talk about something personal rather than a work related issue is not going to learn to trust you. Instead, the employee is going to get the impression they are doing your work because you didn't want to do it yourself, and you knew they would get it done for you rather than risk getting into trouble. Trust is always a two-way street, thus you need to maintain it.

Coach employees based on how they work

You may need to coach certain employees more than others. Someone who is taking on a new task under your direction, may need more time and more

44

involvement from you. Once they learn and deeply understand the process, you may not have to coach them as much the next time around. Coaching is also about how you speak with that person. You always need to be respectful, but with some employees you can simply ask for something specific, as with others you may need to speak more respectfully, with more authority behind the request.

Monitor the person at each stage

Monitoring the person at each stage of a new project is not about a lack of trust or coaching. It is to keep you apprised of what is going on. What if a client calls and wants to know how their project is coming along, but you haven't monitored any of the stages in the process. A successful owner or executive monitors the important stages, so they are not caught off-guard by a client. It does not take long to monitor what has been delegated enough to ensure you know what is going on. Many successful businesses like Wal-mart were built on the owner coming into the first store, saying hello to the employees, looking around, and going about their more important tasks. It is a process that still works.

« Chapter 6 »

How to get the Goals you want to Achieve

Reaching your goals is a continual process, like running a business successfully is a process that needs continual evaluation to keep up with the changes of time. You are always going to work on your business skills to meet the demands of the business you are in. Even after you understand how to accomplish what matters, you need to continue working towards new goals.

You will have business and personal goals to achieve. If you are a manager, your next long term goal may be to become an owner of your own company. A short term goal would be how to achieve that goal such as gaining the skills, education, and work history.

Write your goals down

Whether you are setting business or personal goals for your career desires you need to write them down—always. By writing out your goals, you have something to refer back to when times become a little tough. You also have a record to go back to and change. You may need to add a new skill or education point that will help you achieve your goal. It can be added to the list you have written down. It does not matter how you write it down, but here are a few ways successful business people have:

- A piece of cardboard or poster board, with long term and short term goals written in bubbles or in a list. A poster board is large and can be set up for easy viewing.

- A journal is more private, but just as easy to examine.

You could use a computer to write your goals out; however, there is one thing many successful business individuals of the non-computer eras will tell you—holding a piece of paper is more tangible. There is something about holding the paper or poster board with your goals that makes it more real than seeing it displayed on a computer screen.

Business goals are achieved with employees

Personal goals are great. If you are running the company, you also need to have business goals. These goals are attainable because every employee is dedicated to making them happy. This is where the delicate balance of respect, trust, and company structure will become imperative for reaching the goals you want to achieve in business.

- Have a method to evaluate the responsibility of employees and you

- Be effective, respectful, and maintain rules

- Maintain the process you have in place

- Employee Persuasion

You will need to have a company structure in place for evaluating the responsibilities of all employees and yourself. In this way, you have tangible information to determine if everyone is doing their part to achieve the goals you have set forth. As with delegating and sales goals, you have overall business goals that need to be met through team work. Everyone must be held accountable for the tasks they are assigned, in order for the goals to be achieved. It goes back to the incentivized goals you create in your company.

You and your employees are more likely to achieve the goals when there is a reason to do so. Being evaluated can be an incentive. Most individuals do not want a negative review of their effectiveness, thus they are apt to fulfill their responsibilities.

Achieving goals is also dependent on your manner and that of all managers. Being effective is only a part of goal reaching methods, as you also need to be respectful and maintain the rules you have set forth.

In business, there should be no "do as I say, not as I do" mentality. You worked hard to reach management or ownership. You have to maintain the rules you have set and be respectful of others.

If you can maintain the processes you have in place, you are more apt to achieve the overall business goals than not. Sometimes you set goals that are unreachable due to changes in the economy or other events you could not forecast. However, it does not mean you give up on the process that has continually worked for you.

You may modify it to fit the changing situation, but never give up completely and revamp the entire system. You have to have confidence in yourself and your business and in your employees to reach the business goals you have set.

Employee Persuasion

Employees need to be persuaded to reach their goals. You do not want your employees to assume cash rewards, parties, lunches, and bonuses are always going to be available. As you learned to be persuasive in meetings and with clients, you also need to be persuasive with employees to reach your company goals.

Persuasion with employees can be filled with small talk about the company, the business goals, and your personal goals within the company.

Successful business people know how to communicate with a variety of individuals, including how to recognize it is important to make employees feel worthwhile.

Think back on a time you held a menial position in a company or held your first job. You might have felt you were doing an excellent job, but never received kudos for it. For a time, this may have affected how willing you were to do something for your managers.

Keeping yourself human in the eyes of employees with persuasive small talk, ensures they are ready for the tasks and goals you have established for them. The person may not want to reach these goals because the company headquarters requires it, or because it is the company goals that you and everyone else created— they may desire to reach the goals simply because of your gift of persuasion.

Checks and Balances

Your company structure for maintaining and reaching goals requires checks and balances for every person. Lower level employees need to know they can come to you when there is a problem.

There is a hierarchy in place, yet sometimes the person above the employee coming to see you may have an issue with their direct supervisor. Your company environment should be created in such a way that there is no fear in coming to a different person out of the hierarchy to deal with a problem. The company structure should not make this an acceptable practice all the time; however, it should be a comfortable environment for those happenstances.

Bringing personal and business goals together

Setting up personal and business goals is done, now you need to create a match between the two. Confidence is an essential part to maintaining and achieving both goals in tandem. You need to have the confidence in the goals you set. The goals should be a little hard to reach, but not unattainable.

Always remember the number one rule: developing the business skills you need is a continual process due to the changing times. You have to continue your education through reading various materials, practicing the concepts in this book, and focusing on your goals. Continue to set goals. Once you achieve a short term goal, set another, and so forth until the long term goal is achieved. After the long term goal is achieved create another. For business goals it is often about the yearly calendar, where you have sales, budget, and marketing goals to reach throughout the year.

Your determination, forming the correct team, and setting goals is the path to achieving success.

Conclusion

Thank you again for purchasing this book!

We hope this book was able to help you in your needs and to satisfy your reading pleasures.

Finally, if you enjoyed this book, please take the time to share your thoughts and post a review on Amazon. It would be greatly appreciated!

Thank you and good luck!

Check Out Our Other Books

Please feel free to visit www.ecarepublishing.com to discover other books we have available.

We would be honored if you participated in our email notifications where you can get early bird announcements of our new upcoming books.

www.ingramcontent.com/pod-product-compliance
Lightning Source LLC
Chambersburg PA
CBHW021444170526
45164CB00001B/379